RUSTY'S SONG

by Milo Mason
illustrated by Lee Lee Brazeal

MODERN CURRICULUM PRESS
Pearson Learning Group

This is a story about two friends named Rusty and the Old Cowboy.

Rusty was called Rusty because her fur was the color of a rusty nail.

The Old Cowboy was called the Old Cowboy because that's exactly what he was.

The Old Cowboy and Rusty had a good life. They just drifted here and there, looking at the scenery. At night by the campfire, Rusty would doze while the Old Cowboy wrote in his diary.

That diary must have held all the Old Cowboy's thoughts and dreams. He didn't talk and never had. Not a word. And no one knew why.

Rusty didn't talk either, but what would you expect from a dog? What Rusty could do, though, was better than talking.

Rusty could sing. She didn't sing words, of course, but it was amazing what that dog could do with yelps, howls, and whines. Why, Rusty sang so well she sounded almost human— only better.

Her singing was soft and gentle. It drifted to you like a cloud. All of Rusty's songs were sad, but that's the way a cowboy likes his singing—sad.

It was strange. But Rusty's singing always made her old pal happy.

Beans
½ off

The Old Cowboy and Rusty never
had much money. You don't need much
when you sleep under the stars and all
you eat is beans.

But even beans cost something. And
when the money ran out, they couldn't
buy more. The first day wasn't so bad.
Anybody can go a day without food. The
day after that was okay too.

By the third day, though, they were feeling bad. They needed money and they needed money right away.

Then the Old Cowboy saw a sign. The town was holding a singing cowboy contest. First prize was one hundred dollars. That sign triggered an idea in the Old Cowboy's head. He studied it for a long time. Then he studied Rusty.

Before long, he had a plan. He was determined to win that contest money.

Singing Cowboy Contest Today!!! First Prize $100

Sometimes plans don't work out. The contest judge shook his head.

"No dogs allowed!" he said. "This here's a singing cowboy contest, not a singing *cowdog* contest."

The Old Cowboy wanted to say that wasn't fair. He wanted to say a cowdog is as good as a cowboy. He wanted to say it's the singing that counts.

But of course he didn't say a thing. He never did.

The Old Cowboy figured he had no other choice. He signed himself up for the contest.

The judge said, "Old Cowboy, how are you going to sing? You can't even talk!"

The Old Cowboy just looked at the judge and didn't say a word.

The contest was that very night. Too soon, it was the Old Cowboy's turn to sing.

His hands began to tremble.

His knees began to knock.

He walked out onto the stage.

Someone hit a switch and the spotlight came on.

The crowd waited. The Old Cowboy looked horrified, but he opened his mouth to sing. The audience leaned forward.

What happened next was awful. Nothing came out of the Old Cowboy's mouth. Not so much as a peep! He tried and tried, but he just couldn't squeeze out a sound.

The audience began to laugh. Then they began to boo.

The Old Cowboy shut his mouth. He hung his head. Rusty hated to see her friend unhappy. So she did the only thing she could to make him feel better.

Rusty started singing.

As soon as they heard Rusty's song, the crowd fell silent. It was just as though someone had flipped a switch. No one coughed, sneezed, or moved.

Rusty sang the saddest song she knew. She sang it better than she had ever sung before. Her song soared out of her throat and drifted over the audience. It was the prettiest song anyone had ever heard.

Rusty's song was so sad and pretty it made everyone in town want to cry. That cowdog song just triggered something in them. It was a sight to see. Grown men's lips began to tremble. Rusty sang louder. Then the crowd started to bawl like babies.

When Rusty finished, all
the folks jumped to their feet
and cheered.

The Old Cowboy grinned from
ear to ear. He clapped until his
hands were sore. Then he gave that
dog a big old hug.

The judge wiped his eyes and
blew his nose.

"Well," he said, "maybe it's
against the rules, but so what? Who
cares if you're a cowdog instead of a
cowboy? If you sing as well as that,
it doesn't matter a lick if you're
an elephant! Rusty, you win
first prize!"

Rusty and the Old Cowboy did their shopping, and then they drifted out of town. The Old Cowboy had a wonderful new tale to write in his diary that night. And if he was happy, Rusty was happy too.

Life was looking mighty fine.

A hundred dollars can buy a lot of beans.

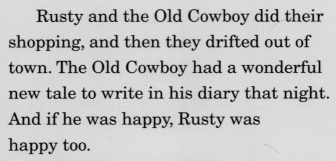